WHAT WAS SAID AT THE BURNS SUPPER

SPEECHES ABOUT ROBERT BURNS
AND REALLY BAD SCOTTISH JOKES
BEST WASHED DOWN WITH A WEE DRAM

By Alan McColl

Published by Mission Point Press
2554 Chandler Rd.
Traverse City, MI 49696
(231) 421-9513
www.MissionPointPress.com

Design by Sarah Meiers

ISBN: 978-1-958363-37-9
Library of Congress Control Number:
2022914806

Printed in the United States of America

WHAT WAS SAID AT THE BURNS SUPPER

SPEECHES ABOUT ROBERT BURNS
AND REALLY BAD SCOTTISH JOKES
BEST WASHED DOWN WITH A WEE DRAM

By Alan McColl

MISSION POINT PRESS

Contents

INTRODUCTION

Over a period of several years, at the Burns Suppers of our local St. Andrews Society in Traverse City, Michigan, I had the opportunity to both give the Immortal Memory speech and, in different years, to be Master of Ceremonies (MC) for the event.

Being MC was really an excuse to tell some bad jokes while keeping the program moving along, and, as the bad jokes were used up, even worse ones were presented at the next occasion. Believe it or not, there are only a certain number of Scottish jokes in bad taste, so many had to be repeated over the years. Similarly, while writing the Immortal Memory speeches, there had to be a certain amount of repetition.

If my last speech were two years previous, then I could hope that few people would remember the jokes or snippets of poems and songs. As it turned out, familiarity with the jokes or works of Burns created an atmosphere where the attendees wanted to hear the same poems and jokes again and again. Must be something weird about the Scots and Scots-wannabes that they will laugh at the same kilt jokes many times.

I have captured in this book my speeches and program notes as MC. I suggest reading a chapter at a time — then you will not suffer from too much repetition. Have a dram as you read — then you will not remember the repetitions from the previous chapter.

Obviously much of the content of my speeches is public record. Poems and songs from Burns are legitimate works of Burns... except Burns was both an author and a collector of Scottish literature. Some works attributed to Burns may have been from what he collected in his travels, and some of the works that he collected may have actually been written by him, especially some of the more risqué sections. Those who appreciate Scottish literature should be eternally grateful that Burns was not only a great author but also for the work he did to collect Scottish folklore for all eternity.

Have I plagiarized? Not intentionally. The closest that I remember was in my first Immortal Memory. Our society president had purchased a downloaded package of Immortal Memory toasts and replies speeches to fit a variety of speech givers. All very appropriate but as dry as two-day-old scones. Somewhere deep on the internet, I found a very interesting speech given by a Canadian woman with an Italian name, who resided deep in Yukon Territory and who previously had very little knowledge of Burns and his works. Her marvelous speech inspired me, and although I did not plagiarize, I made use of her style while writing my own speech. My apologies if there was plagiarizing, but I give sincere thanks for the inspiration she provided.

I said this lady inspired me. Bear in mind that I was, at best, an average student in Scotland's educational system. We did study some of Burns' work — mainly *To a Mouse* and *Tam O'Shanter*. They were fine but just another lesson in school. And Burns might have remained in the background if it had not been for this lady. Yes, my wife and I would attend our local St. Andrews Society Burns Suppers, but that was just part of the Scottish heritage. Writing my own Immortal Memory changed everything. I could not just read someone else's speech — I had to do my own research. I had enough books of Burns in the house, and the internet made things so much easier. I found more poems. I found more stories. My imagination was awakened. And the first speech led to the second, and the second led…

In my first speech, I imagined standing in the toon square telling a stranger all about the infamous Robert Burns. It contains a lot of love poems and talks about Burns' loving relationships with women.

In the second speech, I found a way to talk about the Scottish influence on American Black culture, even bringing in rap music (though I cannot rap). I had known that there were some risqué works by Burns but had never delved into them. Finding *The Merry Muses of Caledonia* was enlightening. This speech was intended to be more adult, maybe a pub session, and contained quite a few risqué verses. I mean, who does not like a dirty ditty?

I was on a roll. What would be the next scene? How about the drawing room in a middle-class merchant's house when the ladies gathered for a glass of sherry and Robert Burns is the guest? What decorum? What swooning! What built-up passions would be released in the home that night? It was never stated that way, but the insinuations were subtly there.

The fourth speech was the courtroom with Robert Burns on trial for debauchery. Obviously guilty, but how would he get out of it? The ghosts of past lovers were not phantoms. No hate or animosity for the former lover.

That concluded my four-part series, but I was asked one more time to make a speech, and it was at an emotional time in my life. A very good friend had just died, and I had been allowed to give a eulogy in which I adapted two songs to make them personal for my late friend. In such melancholy, I decided to speak at the Burns Supper about memories, farewells, and passing. There was a lot of material available, some about former lovers of Burns and some about everlasting love. It did not fit my normal pattern, but life is not always full of jokes and joy.

It is all very well and good to think about Burns in the past as an eighteenth century enlightenment author somewhat ahead of his time. The more you dig into his works, the more you realize his teachings are still very relevant to today.

Some years ago, my niece Sara sent me a poem amongst her other email forwardings that has since become quite famous. "Tae a Fert" is a parody on "To a Haggis," but it is about certain inappropriate body functions. This poem was my bridge to the present. And so, in some of my speeches, I would mention the spirit of Burns being alive today and writing this parody. I did not include this in every speech because too much of a good thing can curdle its audience. If my last usage was several years ago, then it could be repeated. If you can still hold your audience in rapt attention, then a good recital can bring rapture. There has been no better feeling than having the audience rolling in the aisles and especially to pointing out someone at relevant moments while everyone else laughs and is thankful that the finger is not pointing at them. As far as I can tell, this parody has no copyright, so I feel free to use it. Somewhat selfishly, however, I prefer not to pass it on to others. I want to be the one to read it aloud for them.

My objective in each speech or MC program was to keep the event moving along without anyone being bored. I wanted the most entertainment value possible. As such, I tried to minimize long paragraphs of opinions and dry reading and to instead find passion and humour in Burns' works.

My family moved around a bit while I was growing up until we moved to St. Andrews when I was twelve. A small town with its university filled with English students is not exactly the place to develop a broad Scots dialect. I suppose that, like Burns, most of us Scots can somewhat speak in either clear English or Lowland Scots, the latter much diluted from the days of Burns. Back in the 1990s, there was a film with some broad Scots accents, *Four Weddings and a Funeral*, that my wife and I were watching at home. We took a break halfway through, and we conversed. My wife noticed that I had picked up the Scottish accent without realizing it. In my speeches, I try to put myself into the Scots tongue through my standard "Jimmie/hen" introduction. I do not declare my speech-giving accent is pure, but it serves the purpose of presenting a Scottish speech that captures the essence of the subject matter. Similarly, in the written word, I have taken license to spell some Scots words somewhat phonetically as a reminder to pour the accent on as thick as lemon curd.

JANUARY 2008 —
The Toon Square

In which, standing in the toon square, we tell a stranger all about Robert Burns.

Sae, ha's it goin', Jimmie?
Ar' ye' a' right then, hen?

You dinna mind if a' just blether here a wee bit? Wanna tell you a story about this young Scots lad. Rabbie Burns was a po' plo' boy. Dinna hae much more than a penny to haes name. Just like his faither a'fore him who was a tenant fermer. Dem Yankees wo'd prob'ly just call 'em sharecroppers.

Ah, but po Rabbie hae many ither thin's goin' for him, an maybe not aw for the good. Yu see, young Rabbie had a thin' for the lasses, and the lassies seem to hae a thin' for him as'weel. An mony's the young lass who paid for her meeschief w' some shame on 'er famly an' bein' sent away to hae her bairn. Now, Rabbie was nae the typ of guy to wak awa frae a guid thin', and he us'ully cam back for mair as soon as he could, e'en if that meant sae more bairns comin' about efterwrds.

Ah Rabbie, Ah Rabbie, Thou'll get thy fairin',
In Hell they'll roast thee like a herrin'!

Rabbie was born near Ayr on January 25, 1759. His parents were William and Agnes Burnes. Tho' poor, Rabbie was ge'en an educashion and lerned to read and write in both English and Lowland Scots. Burns wrote much of his story in English.

He says: "My father was advanced in life when he married; I was the eldest of seven children; and he, worn out by early hardships, was unfit for labour. We lived very poorly; I was a dexerous ploughman for my age."

Regarding his schooling, Burns says, "Though it cost the schoolmaster some thrashings, I made an excellent English scholar. I was a good deal noted for a retentive memory."

At fifteen, Rabbie was smitten with his first love — young Nellie Kirkpatrick, who was helping with the harvest on his faither's farm. "Handsome Nell" was his first attempt at rhyme:

O, once I lov'd a bonny lass
An' aye I love her still
An' whilst that virtue warms my breast,
I'll love my handsome Nell.

A bonny lass, I will confess,
Is pleasant to the e'e,
But without some better qualities,
She's no a lass for me.

> She dresses aye sae clean and neat,
> Baith decent and genteel;
> And then there's something in her gait
> Gars ony dress look weel.

At the age of seventeen, he put his feelings to paper for Alison Begbie:

> But it's not her air, her form, her face,
> Tho' matching beauty's fabled queen;
> 'Tis the mind that shines in ev'ry grace
> An' chiefly in rogueish een.

At the young age of seventeen, he already knew to appreciate a woman for her mind. But by now, there was no stoppin' Rabbie Burns and his love o' the lasses. As he 'imsel' described it:

> There's ae wee faut they whiles lay to me,
> I like the lasses - Gude forgie me!
> For mony a plack they wheedle frae me
> At dance or fair;
> Maybe some ither things they gie me,
> They weel can spare.

Burns went on to hae many local affairs. He had a dochter with Lizzie Paton, his mither's servant lass. He was also after Jean Armour at that time, who also became pregnant, and her family sent her awa'. He wrote "Of a' the Airts" for Jean (airts means directions):

Of a' the airts the wind can blaw,
I dearly like the west,
For there the bonie lassie lives,
The lassie I lo'e best:
There wild woods grow, and rivers row
and mony a hill between;
but day and night my fancy's flight
is ever wi' my Jean.

I see her in the dewy flowers,
I see her sweet and fair:
I hear her in the tunefu' birds,
I hear her charm the air:
There's not a bonie flower that springs
by fountain, shaw, or green;
there's not a bonie bird that sings,
but minds me o my Jean.

So, he got involved wi' Mary Campbell, wha he appears to hae deeply loved. She may hae died in childbirth. He wrote the poem "Highland Mary" in her memory:

Wi' mony a vow, and lock'd embrace,
Our parting was fu' tender
And, pledging aft to meet again,
We tore oursels asunder;
But, Oh! Fell Death' untimely frost,
That nipt my flower sae early!
Now, Green's the sod, and cauld's the clay,
That wraps my Highland Mary!

His first book of poetry became an overnight sensation, an' he returned home to court Jean Armour again. Despite her parents' disapproval, Burns stayed wi' her during her second pregnancy.

Then it was on to Agnes Craig M'lehose, known to her friends as Nancy. Burns wrote "Ae Fond Kiss" as a memorial to his final parting with her:

> Ae fond kiss and then we sever;
> Ae fareweel, alas, for ever!
> Deep in heart-wrung tears I'll pledge thee,
> Warring sighs and groans I'll wage thee.
> Who shall say that fortune grieves him
> While the star of hope she leaves him?
> Me, nae cheerfu' twinkle lights me,
> Dark despair around benights me.
>
> I'll ne'er blame my partial fancy,
> Naething could resist my Nancy;
> But to see her was to love her,
> Love but her, and love for ever.
> Had we never lov'd sae kindly,
> Had we never lov'd sae blindly,
> Never met - or never parted,
> We had ne'er been broken hearted.

And then, to end the afternoon, he recited part of an auld traditional song:

> There's nought but care on ev'ry han',
> In ev'ry hour that passes, O;
> What signifies the life o' man,
> An' 'twere na for the lasses, O?
>
> Green grow the rashes, O!
> Green grow the rashes, O!
> The sweetest hours that e'er I spend,
> Are spent amang the lasses, O!
>
> For you sae douse, ye sneer at this,
> Ye're nought but senseless asses, O;
> The wisest man the warld e'er saw,
> He dearly lov'd the lasses, O.
>
> Auld Nature swears, the lovely dears
> Her noblest work she classes, O:
> Her 'prentice han' she tried on man,
> An' then she made the lasses, O.
>
> Green grow the rashes, O!
> Green grow the rashes, O!
> The sweetest hours that e'er I spend,
> Are spent amang the lasses, O!

Annie had long since returned to the drawing room and had even retained enough composure to put more coals on the fire. At her dame's signal, after Burns had been thanked by the ladies, Annie showed Mr. Burns out of the room. The ladies sighed collectively, most dabbing their skins with fresh handkerchiefs. This had never happened before. Mistress Balfour had certainly exceeded their expectations with the entertainment. The local bookseller would be selling many copies of Burns' Kilmarnock Edition in the next few days, and certain husbands and suitors had better make some improved romantic efforts if they were to retain their lover's affections.

Mistress Balfour rang her bell for Annie to come back for some service. "Whaur's that lassie, noo?" she declared when no one came.

Now is the time to raise your glasses and rise. I offer a toast. To our poet o' a' the ages. To Scotland's best-lo'ed son. To the Immortal Memory of Robert Burns!

The Court

In which Robert Burns is tried for debauchery.

"Order in the court!" cried out the bailiff. "The right honorable James C. Patterson, Esq. presiding over the Sheriff Court in the county of Ayr. Long live King George."

Everyone in the crowded court stood as James Patterson entered the court and took his seat. "What is the first order of business?"

"The case against Robert Burns. The defendant is charged with debauchery, loose morals, and leading young women astray. The church has already found the defendant guilty, and he was sentenced to sit in the corner stool for four Sundays."

"How do you plead, Mr. Burns?" demanded the judge.

> Ye see yon birkie ca'd a lord,
> Wha struts, an' stares, an' a' that;
> Tho' hundreds worship at his word,
> He's but a coof for a' that.
> For a' that, an' a' that,

His ribband, star, an' a' that,
The man o' independent mind
He looks an' laughs at a' that.

"That is not very helpful, Mr. Burns," said the judge, confused about whether our Rabbie was pleading or insulting the court process. "Are the witnesses all present? And bailiff, why are all these bairns screaming and running around? Is this no a court of law?" he continued.

"These are the bairns belonging to the witnesses and may themselves be introduced as evidence," responded the bailiff. The judge sighed. Traveling doon from Glesga' was never an easy trip, and the pay for attending court was less than he could make in his advocate practice.

"Mr. Burns, did you know a Miss Nelly Kilpatrick, and, if so, how would you describe your relationship?"

Burns replied:

The lasses staw frae 'mang them a'
To pou their stalks of corn:
But Rab slips out, and jinks about,
Behint the muckle thorn:
He grippet Nelly hard and fast;
Loud skirl'd a' the lasses;
But her tap-pickle maist was lost,
When kitlin' in the fause-house
Wi' him that night.

"Miss Kilpatrick, does this refer to you?" asked the judge.

"I would not know, sir. I have not heard this before, and it would not be appropriate to say in public."

"Mr. Burns, do you have anything to say?" asked the judge.

Rabbie spoke up:

> O once I lov'd a bonny lass,
> Aye, and I love her still;
> And whilst that virtue warms my breast,
> I'll love my handsome Nell.

"Mr. Burns, did you know a Miss Peggy Thompson, and, if so, how would you describe your relationship?"

> Peggy was my Deity for six or eight months.

And then he went on:

> I met with my Angel ... It was vain to think of doing any more good at school. The remaining week I staid, I did nothing but craze the faculties of my soul about her or steal out to meet with her; and the two last nights of my stay in the country, had sleep been a mortal sin, I was innocent. I returned home very considerably improved.

"Miss Thompson, based on the charges against Mr. Burns, do you accept or deny these comments?"

After Peggy quietly, and with a tear in her eye, acknowledged the situation, the judge asked our Rabbie if he had anything to say.

We'll gently walk, and sweetly talk,
Till the silent moon shine clearly;
I'll grasp thy waist, and, fondly prest,
Swear how I love thee dearly:
Not vernal show'rs to budding flow'rs,
Not autumn to the farmer,
So dear can be as thou to me,
My fair, my lovely charmer!

"Mr. Burns, did you know a Miss Alison Begbie, sometimes known as Miss Elizabeth Gebbie, and, if so, how would you describe your relationship, and was there a proposal written?" The judge by this time should have been on his fifth case and did not ask why the name confusion.

Rabbie replied, reading from a slip of paper he removed from a pocket:

If you will be so good and so generous as to admit me for your partner, your companion, your bosom friend through life, there is nothing on this side of eternity shall give me greater transport.

"And you were rejected?" asked the judge.

"Yes, Y're Honor."

"And how would you describe your relationship with Miss Begbie?"

On Cessnock banks a lassie dwells,
Could I describe her shape and mien!
Our lasses a' she far excels,
An she has twa sparkling, rogueish een!
But it's not her air, her form, her face,
Tho matching beauty's fabled queen:
'Tis the mind that shines in ev'ry grace—
An chiefly in her rogueish een!

While the judge checked some notes, a child made a noise.

"Whose child is that? What is the mother's name?"

"Elizabeth Paton," came a voice from the back of the courtyard.

"Who is the faither of this Bairn?" asked the judge.

"Rabbie Burns, sir," she replied.

"And what support has he provided?"

"He paid twenty pounds, but that was a yair after her birth, and he had to pay a guinea to the poor box and make penance in front of the congregation," went on young Elizabeth.

"Mr. Burns?"

Welcome! my bonie, sweet, wee dochter,
Tho' ye come here a wee unsought for,
And tho' your comin' I hae fought for,
Baith kirk and queir;
Yet, by my faith, ye're no unwrought for,
That I shall swear!

Lord grant that thou may aye inherit
Thy mither's person, grace, an' merit,
An' thy poor, worthless daddy's spirit,
Without his failins,
'Twill please me mair to see thee heir it,
Than stockit mailens.

Next to be called was Jean Armour. After Burns was asked about his relationship with the same question, now about Jean Armour, he stated:

"O Jeanie fair, I lo'e thee dear;
O canst thou think to fancy me,
Or wilt thou leave thy mammie's cot,
And learn to tent the farms wi' me?"

Now what could artless Jeanie do?
She had nae will to say him na:
At length she blush'd a sweet consent,
And love was aye between them twa.

Miss Armour was called to testify about their relationship.

"Y're Honor, we ha'ed a marriage certificate, but ma faither destroyed it and sent me away to Paisley," she said.

The judge asked, "Was there anything else the court should know about this relationship?"

"Y're Honor, I was expectin a bairn at the time, and the kirk summoned me back to Mauchline to confess that the faither was Robert Burns."

"Mr. Burns," the judge continued, "did you know of and have a relationship with Mary Campbell?"

Burns replied:

> Wi' mony a vow, and lock'd embrace,
> Our parting was fu' tender
> And, pledging aft to meet again,
> We tore oursels asunder;
> But, Oh! Fell Death' untimely frost,
> That nipt my flower sae early!
> Now, Green's the sod, and cauld's the clay,
> That wraps my Highland Mary!

The judge, pretty exasperated with this case, the complexity, and the way the defendant never answered questions directly, decided to move things along quicker.

"Mr. Burns, I have reports here about relationships, some resulting in out of wedlock bairns, with Agnes Craig M'lehose, Jenny Clow, Mary Cameron, and with Anna Park. What do you say?"

> Ae fond kiss and then we sever;
> Ae fareweel, alas, for ever!
> Deep in heart-wrung tears I'll pledge thee,
> Warring sighs and groans I'll wage thee.
> Who shall say that fortune grieves him
> While the star of hope she leaves him?
> Me, nae cheerfu' twinkle lights me,
> Dark despair around benights me.

The judge spoke: "The allegations against the defendant, as confirmed by the evidence, by documentation from the kirk, by the witnesses present, and by the words of the defendant himself confirm the guilt of the defendant, Robert Burns. It is the court's finding that the defendant is a danger to the women of Scotland and that the court must find the defendant guilty and sentence him to…"

"Y're Honor, Y're Honor!" cried out a voice in the court, as one of the witnesses rose, shouting loudly.

"Silence, silence!" declared the judge, "As I was saying, sentence him to…" He was again cut off.

"Y're Honor, Y're Honor!"

"Shall I find you in contempt, woman?" called the judge.

"No, Y're Honor, may I say something?"

"Well, it appears I am not going to be saying anything until you are silenced. Who are you, and what do you want?"

"Alison Begbie, Y're Honor," she said. "If it pleases the court, and my understanding of the law is far inferior to Y're Honor, but the only legal sentence for a single man in these situations is banishment to Jamaica. Y're Honor, all of us of the female gender here today hae lo'd Rabbie dearly. Sorry, Mr. Burns. We did sae on oor own affair and accept the consequences. Hoo'e'r, Miss Armour was really his only true love, and there was a marriage certificate at one time. So, if it pleases the court, could the case be adjourned a wee while, and Mr. Burns and Miss Armour could make their relationship official, if you see what I mean?"

"Court remanded for lunch!" the judge hammered his gavel, stood, and walked out.

One ending of this story could be Burns taking care of the situation. Another would have him waking from this nightmare, returning to Mauchline from Edinburgh where his Kilmarnock Edition had been selling well, and finding his Bonnie Jean destitute, having been made homeless by her faither. Anyway, he married her. I wish we could say there were no more affairs, but that is not the case. But there were nine children born to the Burns family. And Burns did write this to his wife, Jean:

Then come, sweet muse, inspire my lay!
For a' the lee-lang simmer's day
I couldna sing, I couldna say,
How much how dear I love thee.
I see thee dancing o'er the green,
Thy waist sae jimp, thy limbs sae clean,
Thy tempting lips, thy roguish een-
By Heav'n and Earth I love thee!

So, this is our hero, described as a roguish fellow. So charmin', but so brazen.

Now is the time to raise your glasses and rise. I offer a toast. To our poet o' a' the ages. To Scotland's best-lo'ed son. To the Immortal Memory of Robert Burns!

JANUARY 2020 —

Passings

In which we remember auld acquaintances.

Sae, ha's it goin', Jimmie?
Ar' ye' a' right then, hen?

Well, if you ha'd been here last year when I spoke, you'd could have heard whit I ca' the "adult version" of my talk. (That was an edited version of the 2011 speech.) Got pretty raunchy, but apairt from Donald here, most folks wouldna' have caught what I was blethering about, either cos they was sleeping or didna' understand when I put on my fake Scottish accent. You ken, I really just put it on for you guys to mak me sound more impressive. And of course, you guys see right through me. Ah, well.

So here is one little poem from last year:

Roseberry to his Lady says,
My hinnie and my succar,
O shall we do the thing you ken
Or shall we take our supper?

Wi' modest face, sae full of grace,
Reply'd his bonny Lady,
"My noble Lord, do as you please,
But supper is not ready."

And that will put last year to bed.

On this past Hogmanay, I lost a very dear friend. Andrew Wallace Baker was very proud of his Scottish heritage and was proud to wear his kilt. He liked to attend Celtic concerts and other Scottish cultural events, usually with us. Obviously, this put me in a pretty somber mood for some time, so the rest of this talk will be about farewells and passings. Burns was a master in writing about such things.

He wrote the poem "Highland Mary" in memory of Mary Campbell who may have died in childbirth:

Wi' mony a vow, and lock'd embrace,
Our parting was fu' tender
And, pledging aft to meet again,
We tore oursels asunder;
But, Oh! Fell Death' untimely frost,
That nipt my flower sae early!
Now, Green's the sod, and cauld's the clay,
That wraps my Highland Mary!

Another lover was Agnes Craig M'lehose, known to her friends as Nancy.

Burns wrote "Ae Fond Kiss" as a memorial to his final parting with her:

> Ae fond kiss and then we sever;
> Ae fareweel, alas, for ever!
> Deep in heart-wrung tears I'll pledge thee,
> Warring sighs and groans I'll wage thee.
> Who shall say that fortune grieves him
> While the star of hope she leaves him?
> Me, nae cheerfu' twinkle lights me,
> Dark despair around benights me.
>
> I'll ne'er blame my partial fancy,
> Naething could resist my Nancy;
> But to see her was to love her,
> Love but her, and love for ever.
> Had we never lov'd sae kindly,
> Had we never lov'd sae blindly,
> Never met — or never parted,
> We had ne'er been broken hearted.

Now, some poems are about everlasting love. First, "A Red, Red Rose":

> O, my luve's like a red, red rose,
> That's newly sprung in June:
> My luve's like a melodie,
> That's sweetly play'd in tune.

Burns wrote this epitaph for a fellow in Mauchline where Burns farmed:

> Lament him, Mauchline husbands a'
> He aften did assist ye;
> For if ye staid hale weeks awa',
> Your wives, they ne'er never had miss'd ye.

> Ye Mauchline Bairns, as on ye press pass
> To school in bands thegither
> O tread ye lightly on his grass, -
> Perhaps he was your father.

I won't recite "Auld Lang Syne" now — we can sing it together later — but it is about forgiveness and celebrating old friendships.

Burns was not just a writer of great Scottish poems and songs. He also cared about our Scottish heritage of songs, and he did much work collecting them so we can enjoy them today. This included matching up songs to tunes.

While I was thinking about what to say at my departed friend's memorial service, I was reminded of "The Parting Glass." Burns referred to the air in 1786 as "Good night, and joy be wi' ye a'" when using it to accompany his Masonic lyric "The Farewell," which I read before. I modified this song for Andy, though not many changes were required. I will now recite a traditional version that Burns would have recognized, even though it was written about 150 years before his time. Some say some of the verses refer to a condemned cattle rustler named Armstrong before his execution.

Of all the money that e'er I had
I spent it in good company
And all the harm I've ever done
Alas it was to none but me
And all I've done for want of wit
To mem'ry now I can't recall
So fill to me the parting glass
Good night and joy be to you all

So fill to me the parting glass
And drink a health whate'er befall,
And gently rise and softly call
Good night and joy be to you all

Of all the comrades that e'er I had
They're sorry for my going away
And all the sweethearts that e'er I had
They'd wish me one more day to stay

But since it fell unto my lot
That I should rise and you should not
I gently rise and softly call
Good night and joy be to you all

A man may drink and not be drunk
A man may fight and not be slain
A man may court a pretty girl
And perhaps be welcomed back again

But since it has so ought to be
By a time to rise and a time to fall
Come fill to me the parting glass
Good night and joy be with you all
Good night and joy be with you all

Now is the time to raise your glasses and rise. I offer a toast. To our poet o' a' the ages. To Scotland's best-lo'ed son. To the Immortal Memory of Robert Burns!

Master of Ceremonies
2014

January 26, 2014

Sae, ha's it goin', Jimmie?
Ar' ye' a' right then, hen?

I am Alan McColl, and it is my pleasure, and your con-
dolences, for me to be tonight's Master of Ceremonies. That
means it is my job to come out and make a poor attempt at a
joke anytime there is nothing happening. We have on the back
table here various poems and songs of Burns, and we would
like you to come up and select one to read out over dinner. We
don't mind how well you read; nobody will know. You think
just because I have this accent, I read them correctly? Naw,
the accent is a disguise for misp ron ounce ments.

What's the difference between a Scotsman and a canoe?
A canoe sometimes tips.

How do you know if a Scotsman is left-handed? He keeps all his money in his right-hand pocket.

Did you hear about the Scotsman who washed his kilt? He couldn't do a fling with it.

How do you get a Scotsman to climb onto the roof of his home? Tell him that the drinks are on the house.

Hear about the skeleton that wore a kilt? It was Boney Prince Charlie.

McDougal bought two tickets for the lottery. He won five million pounds.

"How do you feel about your big win?" asked a newspaper reporter.

"Disappointed," said McDougal. "My other ticket didn't win anything."

One day Jock bought a bottle of fine whiskey, and, while walking home, he fell. Getting up, he felt something wet on his pants. He looked up at the sky and said, "Oh lord, please, I beg you — let it be blood!"

A Scots Toast

May the best you've ever seen
Be the worst you'll ever see;
May the mouse ne'er leave your girnal
Wi' a tear drap in its e'e;
May your lum keep blithely reekin'
Till ye're auld enough to dee;
May you aye be just as happy
As I wish you now to be!

Burns at the Farmyard

Robert Burns and his brother Gilbert were leaning over a farmyard wall, watching the hens and the cockerel scratching about.

One of the hens gives the cockerel the eye, and he starts to strut across the yard to do his manly duty.

Just then, the farmer comes out and scatters seed about the yard. The cockerel stops and starts to peck at the seed.

On seeing this Rabbie turns to his brother and says, "Gilbert, I pray I will never be as hungry as that."

So, why are we here to immortalize Rabbie Burns? He was just a simple plowman. Well, yea, he did write a lot of quite good poetry and songs. But he was a man of the people. He was well loved in his time and even today. The lassies loved him. Boy, did they ever, and many's the bairn he fathered.

And they guys in the pubs loved him when he told his stories and sung away the night over drinks. You know, you are going to hear a lot of his works tonight. They are deep. They are about everyday things. They relate to you and me. Enjoy them. Think about them. And later on tonight, we will make a toast to his memory.

A Scottish preacher said to his congregation: "I don't mind you putting buttons in the collection plate, but please provide your own buttons. Stop pulling them off the church cushions."

Another Scottish preacher is said to have prayed thus after a particularly unproductive collection: "We thank you, Lord, that the plate was returned safely."

Well, if I am telling preacher jokes, it must be time to invite a preacher to the podium to officially start our proceedings with the Selkirk Grace. Our thanks to the Reverend B.M. for doing this.

Selkirk Grace

> Some hae meat and canna eat,
> And some wad eat that want it;
> But we hae meat, and we can eat,
> Sae let the Lord be thankit.

Seems that a clan chief's daughter was offered as a bride to the son of a neighboring chief in exchange for two cows and four sheep. The big swap was to happen on the shore of the stream that separated the two clans. Father and daughter showed up at the appointed time only to discover that the groom and his livestock were on the other side of the stream. The father grunted, "The fool doesn't know which side his bride is bartered on."

At this time, I would like to introduce Lee and her Celtic Fire Highland dancers for some Scottish dancing.

Dancing

MacTavish visited London for his annual holiday and stayed at a large hotel. However, he didnae feel that the natives were friendly.

"At 4 o'clock every morning," he told a friend, "they hammered on my bedroom door, on the walls, and even on the floor and ceiling. Och, sometimes they hammered so loud I could hardly hear myself playing the bagpipes."

A bagpipe joke must be followed by a bagpiper. It is now time to pipe in the haggis. Clyde is our piper, M.A. will carry the haggis, and G.V. will recite the Toast to the Haggis.

Piping in of the Haggis

Toast to the Haggis

(Traditional and English versions of "To a Haggis" are printed at end of book)

Dinner

I would like to introduce Jane, who will play some concertina tunes.

A Scot is emigrating to Australia. Upon entry, he is being interviewed by the immigration officer. The officer asks the question, "Do you have a criminal record?"

The Scot replies, "Well, no. I didn't realize you still needed one to get in!"

I would now like to invite Donald to present his Immortal Memory of Robert Burns. Donald is a recent member of our society, migrating to Northern Michigan from Illinois, where he was a pastor. Before that, he jumped across the Atlantic to a new country. Please have something in your glass for some toasts when he is finished.

Immortal Memory

> Women are beautiful and foolish.
> Beautiful so that men will love them.
> Foolish so that they will love man.

Wee Hughie came into the office an hour late for the third time in one week and found the boss waiting for him. "What's the story this time, Hughie?" he asked sarcastically. "Let's hear a good excuse for a change."

Wee Hughie sighed, "Everything went wrong this morning. The wife decided to drive me to the harbour. She got ready in ten minutes, but then the ferry didn't turn up. Rather than let you down, I swam across the river, ran over the mountain, borrowed a bicycle, and cycled the twenty miles through the glen to this office."

"You'll have to do better than that, Hughie," said his boss, disappointed. "No woman can be ready in ten minutes."

Now I would welcome H.D. to give the Toast to the Lassies. H.D. migrated from the Detroit area and found paradise in Northern Michigan.

Toast to the Lassies

And without any jokes, H.D.'s wife M.D. will now make the Reply from the Lassies.

Reply from the Lassies

McLeod asked the conductor how much the bus fare into the city was.

"Fifteen cents," said the conductor. McLeod thought this was a bit much, so he decided to run behind the bus for a few stops.

"How much is it now?" he gasped.

"Still fifteen cents," said the conductor.

McLeod ran three further stops behind the bus and was barely able to ask the conductor again what the fare was now.

"Twenty cents," said the conductor. "You're running in the wrong direction."

Donald McPherson, a very tight man, was looking for a gift for a friend. Everything was too expensive except for a glass that was broken, which he could buy for almost nothing. He asked the store to send it, hoping his friend would think it had been broken in transit. In due time, he received a reply. "Thanks for the vase," it read. "It was thoughtful of you to wrap each piece separately."

Sandy became depressed and decided to end it all by hanging himself. However, his friend Donald came along in the nick of time, cut the rope, and saved his life. Sandy, true to form, sent Donald a bill for the cost of the rope.

Donald: "I always feel that I'm covered in gold paint, doctor." Psychiatrist: "Oh, that's just your gilt complex."

So, if we are talking about money, cheapness, and gold, it must be time for the raffle.

Raffle

What is the definition of a true Scottish gentleman? A Scotsman who knows how to play the bagpipes but doesn't.

Why do pipers like to march as they play the bagpipes? A moving target is harder to hit.

Why do bagpipers walk when they play? They're trying to get away from the noise.

And that should be a clue that Clyde is ready to play a couple more tunes on the pipes.

Piping

Two American tourists visit a famed Highland distiller. Afterward, they drove towards the city of Edinburgh in a zig-zag pattern.

"Sandy, are we near the city yet?"

"We're knocking down more people, so we must be."

"Drive slower, then."

"Whadda ya mean, drive slower? You're driving."

The MacTavish brothers decided that one of their number would go to America and make his fortune, and then come back to share with the rest of them. The youngest, Ian, was chosen for this task. Off he went, and he worked hard in America and earned himself a fortune over a few years. He wired his brothers that he'd be returning with it.

When he came back to Scotland, he got off the boat and looked around for his brothers, but he could not see anyone who looked familiar. Finally, a group of bearded strangers approached.

"Ho, Ian, are ye not knowing yer own brothers?" asked the first one. Then Ian realized his brothers had grown beards.

"Fer heaven's sake, laddies, what would ye be growin' them beards for, now?" he asked.

"We had to, lad, ye took the razor wi' ye!"

Archie was in poor health. He asked his friend Sandy if he would pour a bottle of whiskey over his grave should he die one of these days.

Sandy said, "Sure'n I'll be glad, laddie, but would you mind if I passed it through my kidneys first?"

We'd now like our society's president, Jim, to come up for some closing words and appreciation, and then we should all stand, join hands, and sing "Auld Lang Syne."

"Auld Lang Syne" ~ English Version

Should auld acquaintance be forgot
And never brought to mind
Should auld acquaintance be forgot
And days of auld lang syne

For auld lang syne my dear
For auld lang syne
We'll take a cup of kindness yet
For auld lang syne

And here's a hand my trusty friend
That gives a hand to thine
We'll take a cup of kindness yet
For auld lang syne

Master of Ceremonies 2015

January 25, 2015

Sae, ha's it goin', Jimmie?
Ar' ye' a' right then, hen?

My name is Alan McColl, and I ask for your patience, as I will be tonight's Master of Ceremonies. That means it is my job to come out and make a poor attempt at a joke anytime there is nothing happening, and I used up all the really bad jokes last year. So, we are really scraping the barrel this year.

A Scots Toast

May the best you've ever seen
Be the worst you'll ever see;
May the mouse ne'er leave your girnal
Wi' a tear drap in its e'e;
May your lum keep blithely reekin'
Till ye're auld enough to dee;

May you aye be just as happy
As I wish you now to be!

Did you hear about the Scotsman who washed his kilt?
He couldn't do a fling with it.

We have on the back table here various poems and songs
of Burns, and we would like you to come up and select one
to read out over dinner. We don't mind how well you read;
nobody will know. You think just because I have this accent,
I read them correctly? Naw, the accent is a disguise for misp
ron ounce ments. I would like to warn you that our young
dancers have been known to give out more complicated poems
to read to those who do not volunteer.

We will be having a fifty/fifty raffle tonight. You can get
six tickets for five dollars or one dollar each.

How do you know if a Scotsman is left-handed? He keeps
all his money in his right-hand pocket.

So, we are on to you if you declare you have no money.

We have all heard about brothers who are total opposites,
like Cain and Abel. There is also Prince William who got the
brunette and his very wild brother Prince Harry. Buckingham
Palace did not know what to do about Harry and eventually
decided for him to split his time between the military and the
royal visits that no one else wanted to do.

One morning, Prince Harry wakes up with the worst
hangover. He has no idea where he is. There are two babes in
his bed. Who they are or why they are there is beyond him.

His head is aching. His valet comes into the room and tells him he is in Glasgow and has twenty-three minutes before his first appointment at the Royal Infirmary. Prince Harry gets there barely in time, blurry, fuzzy, and aching. He does not remember who he is meeting, he just follows them around as he is taken into a ward. He goes up to greet the first patient.

> O wad some power the giftie gie us
> To see oursels as ithers see us
> It wad frae mony a blunder free us,
> An' foolish notion.

"Quite, quite. Very well said," said the prince, turning away and going to the next patient.

> Of a' the airts the wind can blaw,
> I dearly like the west,
> For there the bonie lassie lives,
> The lassie I lo'e best:
> There wild woods grow, and rivers row
> and mony monie a hill between;
> but day and night my fancy's flight
> is ever wi' my Jean.

The prince is getting confused at this, and it is not helping with his hangover. He goes up to the third patient.

> Then let us pray that come it may
> (As come it will for a' that)
> That sense and worth o'er a' the earth
> Shall bear the gree for a' that
> For a' that and a' that
> It's comin' yet for a' that
> That man to man the world o'er
> Shall brithers be for a' that.

Prince Harry turns to the doctor accompanying him and asks, "What sort of ward is this? Is it a mental ward?"

"No," replies the doctor. "It's the Burns unit."

Celebrating Rabbie Burns should be fun. He wrote a lot of serious poems, but he also wrote to make people laugh. Some of his work in *The Merry Muses of Caledonia* is rather risqué. Some poems and songs are best suited to a wild party or a night at the pub. Burns was a man of the people. You are going to hear a lot of his works tonight. Some are deep. Some are about everyday things. They relate to you and me. Enjoy them. Think about how you can remake them for today.

Does anyone here have a cat at home? Does anyone have a cat who is not a good mouser?

Well, let's do a little parody.

> Some hae Cats aboot their hoose,
> And some hae Cats who dinnae mouse
> But we hae cats upon our laps
> So let us all be thankful.

Now, more seriously, we are going to ask G.V. to come up here and read the Selkirk Grace.

Selkirk Grace

A farmer's wife, who was rather stingy with her whisky, was giving her shepherd a drink. As she handed him his glass, she said it was extra good whisky, being fourteen years old.

"Weel, mistress," said the shepherd regarding his glass sorrowfully, "it's very small for its age."

We now would like to introduce some of the smaller people here, but they have big hearts to come out and dance for us. I would like to introduce Lee and her Celtic Fire Highland dancers for some Scottish dancing.

Dancing

The raffle helps to pay for the haggis. Do you know how expensive it is to artificially impregnate the haggis? And then to find a clockwise leaning hill for it to grow up on, and then to find an anti-clockwise hunter to bring home the bird. Otherwise they will just chase each other round the hill. If the plucker thinks he has to shave the fur instead of plucking the feathers, it gets lumpy. And someone's always complaining that they get the short leg — cos' if all the legs were the same length, he would topple over on the hillside. It's not easy to get some haggis for our little Burns Supper.

What did the bagpiper get on his IQ test? Drool.

How can you tell if a bagpipe is out of tune? Someone is blowing into it.

A bagpipe joke has to be followed by a bagpiper. It is now time to pipe in the haggis. Clyde is our piper, R.K. will carry the haggis, and Donald will recite the Toast to the Haggis.

Piping in of the Haggis

Toast to the Haggis

Dinner

I would like to introduce Jane, who will play some harp or concertina tunes.

Raffle

Now time to ask Lee to bring back her dancers. Aren't they wonderful? You would like them to dance again, right?

Dancing

A keen rugby supporter was watching a match against England at Murrayfield. Beside him was the only empty seat in the stadium.

"Whose seat is that?" asked the man on the other side.

"It is my wife's."

"But why isn't she here?"

"She's dead."

"Then, why didn't you give it to one of your friends?"
"They're all at her funeral."

I would now like to invite one of our newer members, B.D., to present his Immortal Memory of Robert Burns. Please have something in your glass for some toasts when he is finished.

Immortal Memory

> Women are beautiful and foolish.
> Beautiful so that men will love them.
> Foolish so that they will love man.

At a cocktail party, one woman said to another, "Aren't you wearing your wedding ring on the wrong finger?"
The other replied, "Yes, I am. I married the wrong man."

A man placed some flowers on the grave of his dearly departed mother and started back toward his car when his attention was diverted to another man kneeling at a grave.
The man seemed to be praying with profound intensity and kept repeating, "Why did you have to die? Why did you have to die? Why did you have to die? Why did you have to die?"
The first man approached him and said, "Sir, I don't wish to interfere with your private grief, but this demonstration of pain is more than I've ever seen before. For whom do you mourn so deeply? A child? A parent?"
The mourner took a moment to collect himself, then replied, "My wife's first husband."

I think that leads into inviting W.S. to give the Toast to the Lassies.

Toast to the Lassies

"I've kissed every woman in this tenement block except one," said an amorous Glaswegian to his friend, just as one of the male residents of the block was passing. The man immediately turned back, went upstairs, and reported this to his wife.

"I wonder who the woman is that this rascal hasn't kissed?" he said.

"Oh," said the wife, "I suppose it'll be that stuck-up Mary McKay on the third floor."

And without any more words from me, Glad will make the Reply from the Lassies.

Reply from the Lassies

What is the definition of a true Scottish gentleman? A Scotsman who knows how to play the bagpipes but doesn't.

And that should be a clue that Clyde is ready to play a couple more tunes on the pipes.

Piping

A ship upon the ocean falls apart in a storm, runs aground on the rocks, and is wrecked. Miraculously, the crew and passengers are able to get to shore.

There are fifteen Irishmen. They get together and work out a way to retrieve the whisky from the ship, then go off and drink it.

There are fifteen Welshmen. They form up a scrum and spend the rest of the day playing rugby.

There are fifteen Englishmen. They sulked and are upset that they have not been introduced to each other, and off they go in every direction to mope on their own.

There are fifteen Scotsmen. They formed twelve separate St. Andrews Societies.

We'd now like to thank everyone who has contributed to our entertainment and organized tonight. We are a small group, but when we all come together as one society, good things are possible.

Also, thanks to our servers — great job — and thanks to Sleder's for letting us party.

Now, as we end the official program, we don't have to go home yet. Jane will bring out her concertina once more and lead us as we stand up, circle the room, hold hands, and sing together "Auld Lang Syne."

Thank you and God Bless the Scots and all who want to be!

Master of Ceremonies 2016

January 24, 2016

Sae, ha's it goin', Jimmie?
Ar' ye' a' right then, hen?

I am Alan McColl, and it is my pleasure, hopefully with your patience, for me to be tonight's Master of Ceremonies. That means it is my job to come out and make a poor attempt at a joke anytime there is nothing happening. I have used up all the really bad jokes the last couple of years. So, from there, it only gets worse.

Why do all Scots have a sense of humour? Because it is free.

How many Scotsmen does it take to change a light bulb? Och! It's no that dark!

Have you heard about the Scotsman who gave a present of fifty pounds each to an Englishman, an Irishman, and a Welshman? Nor has anyone else.

A visitor to an Aberdeen bar was surprised to find the beer only two pence a pint. The barman explained that it was the price to mark the centenary of the pub opening. The visitor noticed, however, that the bar was empty.

"Are the regular customers not enjoying the special prices?" he asked.

To which the barman replied, "They're waiting for the happy hour."

There are four kinds of people that live in Great Britain.

First are the Scots, who hold onto their children and anything else they can get their hands on.

Next are the Welsh, who pray on their knees and on their neighbors.

Then there are the Irish, who don't know what they want, but they'll fight anyone for it.

Last are the English, who consider themselves self-made men, which relieves the Almighty of any responsibility!

A Scots Toast

May the best you've ever seen
Be the worst you'll ever see;
May the mouse ne'er leave your girnal
Wi' a tear drap in its e'e;
May your lum keep blithely reekin'

Till ye're auld enough to dee;
May you aye be just as happy
As I wish you now to be!

After discovering they had won ten million pounds on the National Lottery, Mr. and Mrs. McKenzie sat down to discuss their future.

"After twenty years of washing other people's stairs to earn money," said Mrs. McKenzie, "at last I can throw away my old scrubbing brush."

"Of course, you can," said her husband. "We can easily afford to buy you a new one now."

We will be having a fifty/fifty raffle tonight. You can get six tickets for five dollars or one dollar each.

We have on the back table here various poems and songs of Burns, and we would like you to come up and select one to read out over dinner. We don't mind how well you read; nobody will know. You think just because I have this accent, I read them correctly? Naw, the accent is a disguise for misp ron ounce ments. I would like to warn you that our young dancers have been known to give out more complicated poems to read to those who do not volunteer, but if they do that, they themselves have to recite as well.

A Scottish preacher said to his congregation: "I don't mind you putting buttons in the collection plate, but please provide your own buttons. Stop pulling them off the church cushions."

Another Scottish preacher is said to have prayed thus after a particularly unproductive collection: "We thank you, Lord, that the plate was returned safely."

Well, if I am telling preacher jokes, it must be time to invite Glad to the podium to officially start our proceedings with the Selkirk Grace.

Selkirk Grace

At this time, I would like to introduce Lee and her Celtic Fire Highland dancers for some Scottish dancing.

Dancing

So, why are we here to immortalize Rabbie Burns? He was just a simple plowman. Well, yea, he did write a lot of quite good poetry and songs. But he was a man of the people. He was well loved in his time and even today. The lassies loved him. Boy, did they ever, and many's the bairn he fathered. And they guys in the pubs loved him when he told his stories and sung away the night over drinks. Rabbie wrote about life: living, loving, and even passing. His works, despite the language, are as true today as they were then.

Callum decided to call his father-in-law the "Exorcist" because every time he came to visit, he made the spirits disappear.

What did the bagpiper get on his IQ test? Drool.

How can you tell if a bagpipe is out of tune? Someone is blowing into it.

A bagpipe joke has to be followed by a bagpiper. It is now time to pipe in the haggis. Clyde is our piper; N.C. will carry the haggis, and A.B. will recite the Toast to the Haggis.

Piping in of the Haggis

Toast to the Haggis

Did you hear about the man who gave up making haggis? He didn't have the stomach for it anymore.

Maître d'hôtel: "Are you here for a special occasion?"
Campbell: "Aye, we won the third prize in the annual Robert Burns Contest — a haggis dinner for two."
Maître d'hôtel: "What were the other prizes?"
Campbell: The second prize was a single haggis dinner, and, if you won the first prize, you didnae have to eat the haggis."

Dinner

McDougal bought two tickets for the lottery. He won five million pounds.
"How do you feel about your big win?" asked a newspaper reporter.
"Disappointed," said McDougal. "My other ticket didn't win anything."

So, if we are talking about money, cheapness, and gold, it must be time for the raffle.

Raffle

An Englishman, Irishman, Welshman, and Scotsman were captured while fighting in a far-off foreign land, and the leader of the captors said, "We're going to line you up in front of a firing squad and shoot you all in turn. But first, you each can make a final wish."

The Englishman responds, "I'd like to hear 'God Save The Queen' just one more time to remind me of the auld country, played by the London All Boys Choir. With Morris dancers dancing to the tune."

The Irishman replies, "I'd like to hear 'Danny Boy' just one more time to remind me of the auld country, sung in the style of Daniel O'Donnell, with Riverdance dancers skipping gaily to the tune."

The Welshman answers, "I'd like to hear 'Men of Harlech' just one more time to remind me of the country, sung as if by the Treorchy Male Voice Choir."

The Scotsman says quickly, "I'd like to be shot first."

I would like to introduce Jane, who will play some concertina tunes.

Music

I would now like to invite Clyde to present his Immortal Memory of Robert Burns. I would like to express my appreciation to Clyde, who, in all my years of bad bagpiper jokes, has never pulled out a frozen haggis and pulverized me with it.

Please have something in your glass for some toasts when he is finished.

Immortal Memory

Mary Clancy goes up to Father O'Grady after his Sunday service, and she's in tears.

He says, "So what's bothering you, Mary, my dear?"

She says, "Oh, Father, I've got terrible news. My husband passed away last night."

The priest says, "Oh, that's terrible. Tell me, Mary, did he have any last requests?"

She says, "That he did, Father."

The priest says, "What did he ask, Mary?"

She says, "He said, 'Please Mary, put down that damn gun.'"

"Listen to this, lads," said the man to his mates in the pub. "Last night, when ah wis in here, a burglar broke in tae ma hoose."

"Did he get anything?"

"Aye, a broken nose and two teeth knocked oot. The wife thought it wis me commin in drunk!"

Walter went on a date with his new girlfriend, and they reached the door of her flat just before midnight. When she kissed him goodnight she said, "Be careful on your way home, or someone might rob you of all the money you've saved this evening."

Have you heard about the lecherous Scotsman who lured a girl up to his attic to see his etchings? He sold her four of them.

A Scotsman took a girl for a romantic ride in his taxi. She was so beautiful; he could hardly keep his eye on the meter.

Now I would welcome Donald to give the Toast to the Lassies.

Toast to the Lassies

And without any jokes, Donald's wife Susan will now make the Reply from the Lassies.

Reply from the Lassies

Why do pipers like to march as they play the bagpipes? A moving target is harder to hit.

Why do bagpipers walk when they play? They're trying to get away from the noise.

And that should be a clue that Clyde is ready to play a couple more tunes on the pipes.

Piping

Two American tourists visit a famed Highland distiller. Afterward, they drove towards the city of Edinburgh in a zig-zag pattern.

"Sandy, are we near the city yet?"

"We're knocking down more people, so we must be."

"Drive slower, then."

"Whadda ya mean, drive slower? You're driving."

An Irishman who had too much to drink is driving home from the city one night, and, of course, his car is weaving all over the road. A cop pulls him over.

"So," says the cop to the driver, "where ya been?"

"Why, I've been to the pub of course," slurs the drunk.

"Well," says the cop, "it looks like you've had quite a few to drink this evening."

"I did all right," the drunk says with a smile.

"Did you know," says the cop, standing straight, folding his arms across his chest, "that a few intersections back, your wife fell out of your car?"

"Oh, thank heavens," sighs the drunk. "For a minute there, I thought I'd gone deaf."

Brenda O'Malley is home making dinner, as usual, when Tim Finnegan arrives at her door.

"Brenda, may I come in?" he asks. "I've somethin' to tell ya."

"Of course, you're always welcome, Tim. But where's my husband?"

"That's what I'm here to be telling ya, Brenda. There was an accident down at the Guinness brewery."

"Oh, God, no!" cries Brenda. "Please don't tell me."

"I must, Brenda. Your husband Seamus is dead and gone. I'm sorry." Finally, she looked up at Tim.

"How did it happen, Tim?"

"It was terrible, Brenda. He fell into a vat of Guinness stout and drowned."

"Oh, my dear Jesus! But you must tell me the truth, Tim. Did he at least go quickly?"

"Well, Brenda, no. In fact, he got out three times to pee."

We'd now like our society's president, Jim, to come up for some closing words and appreciation.

Appreciation

Now, we would like everyone to stand up, form a large circle, hold hands and we will sing "Auld Lang Syne."

"Auld Lang Syne"

Master of Ceremonies 2018

January 26, 2018

> Sae, ha's it goin', Jimmie?
> Ar' ye' a' right then, hen?

I am Alan McColl, and it is my pleasure, hopefully with your patience, for me to be tonight's Master of Ceremonies. That means it is my job to come out and make a poor attempt at a joke anytime there is nothing happening. I have really had to scrape the barrel to find some unused jokes, but they seem to keep getting worse and worse. Maybe I should just repeat previous ones since no one remembers, or I could just announce a number to represent a joke. And then you can politely chuckle, or, if you don't remember which joke that was, you can do a belly laugh.

Why do all Scots have a sense of humour? Because it is free.

How many Scotsmen does it take to change a light bulb? Och! It's no that dark!

Nineteen guys go to the cinema. The ticket lady asks, "Why so many of you?"
Jack replies, "The poster said eighteen and over."

Two guys are talking in the pub. One says his daughter asked for a pet spider for her birthday. He checked the pet shop, and they wanted seventy dollars. Forget it, his buddy says, he can get one cheaper off the web.

I was at an ATM the other day. A little old lady asked if I could check her balance, so I pushed her over.

Did you know that statistically, six out of seven dwarfs are not Happy?

Friends of this sexy babe know she always wanted to have a smokin' hot body, but she dies. So, they arrange for a cremation.

There are four kinds of people that live in Great Britain.
First are the Scots, who hold onto their children and anything else they can get their hands on.
Next are the Welsh, who pray on their knees and on their neighbors.
Then there are the Irish, who don't know what they want, but they'll fight anyone for it.
Last are the English, who consider themselves self-made men, which relieves the Almighty of any responsibility!

A Scots Toast

May the best you've ever seen
Be the worst you'll ever see;
May the mouse ne'er leave your girnal
Wi' a tear drap in its e'e;
May your lum keep blithely reekin'
Till ye're auld enough to dee;
May you aye be just as happy
As I wish you now to be!

After discovering they had won ten million pounds on the National Lottery, Mr. and Mrs. McKenzie sat down to discuss their future.

"After twenty years of washing other people's stairs to earn money," said Mrs. McKenzie, "at last I can throw away my old scrubbing brush."

"Of course, you can," said her husband. "We can easily afford to buy you a new one now."

We will be having a fifty/fifty raffle tonight. You can get six tickets for five dollars or one dollar each.

We have on the back table here various poems and songs of Burns, and we would like you to come up and select one to read out over dinner. We don't mind how well you read; nobody will know. You think just because I have this accent, I read them correctly? Naw, the accent is a disguise for misp ron ounce ments. I would like to warn you that our young dancers have been known to give out more complicated poems to read to those who do not volunteer, but if they do that, they themselves have to recite as well.

A young Scots lass starts showing off a very fancy engagement ring to her friends. It soon gets all around town. Her boyfriend is in the bar, and his mate comes up and says, "That was an expensive ring Jennie has been showing around. I thought she wanted one of them big SUVs?"

"Ah, yea," says the boyfriend, "but where am I going to find a fake Range Rover?"

It is time to invite Dawn to the podium to officially start our proceedings with the Selkirk Grace.

Selkirk Grace

So, why are we here to immortalize Rabbie Burns? He was just a simple plowman. Well, yea, he did write a lot of quite good poetry and songs. But he was a man of the people. He was well loved in his time and even today. The lassies loved him. Boy, did they ever, and mony's the bairn he fathered. And they guys in the pubs loved him when he told his stories and sung away the night over drinks. Rabbie wrote about life: living, loving, and even passing. His works, despite the language, are as true today as they were then.

Callum decided to call his father-in-law the "Exorcist" because every time he came to visit, he made the spirits disappear.

Donald is preaching to his congregation: "I don't mind you putting buttons in the collection plate, but please provide your own buttons. Stop pulling them off the church cushions."

After another particularly unproductive collection, Donald is said to have prayed, "We thank you, Lord, that the plate was returned safely."

Donald was making his rounds to parish homes to receive their tithes and offerings. One of his parishioners gave but had a distinctly stingy attitude when parting with his money without receiving something in return. As he put the gift away, Donald commented dryly, "Tha Good Book says tha Lord loves a cheerful giver, but the Presbyterian Church canna be so choosy."

A bagpiper is standing outside Waverly station, all dressed up and ready to play. His case is open on the ground ready for some tips. A sign reads, "Pay or I play."

Pastor and bagpipe jokes — what a combination. It is now time to pipe in the haggis. Clyde is our piper, Donald will recite the Toast to the Haggis, and, after a couple of comedians, we needed a straight lady to restore the decorum, so N.C. will carry the Haggis.

Piping in of the Haggis

Toast to the Haggis

At this time, I would like to introduce Lee and her Celtic Fire Highland dancers for some Scottish dancing.

Dancing

Did you hear about the man who gave up making haggis? He didn't have the stomach for it anymore.

Maître d'hôtel: "Are you here for a special occasion?"
Campbell: "Aye, we won the third prize in the annual Robert Burns Contest — a haggis dinner for two."
Maître d'hôtel: "What were the other prizes?"
Campbell: "The second prize was a single haggis dinner, and, if you won the first prize, you didnae have to eat the haggis."

Dinner

I would like to introduce Jane who will play some concertina tunes.

Music

McDougal bought two tickets for the lottery. He won five million pounds.

"How do you feel about your big win?" asked a newspaper reporter.

"Disappointed," said McDougal. "My other ticket didn't win anything."

So, if we are talking about money, cheapness, and gold, it must be time for the raffle.

Raffle

Have you ever wondered why the Scots hae an inferiority complex with the English? An English actress and a Scottish actress want some work and go to an advertising agency.

"Do you have any gigs?" The agency says yes. They are shooting some ads and send the ladies through to the back office, telling them to each go to a dressing room and get dressed for their different ads.

A few weeks later the ads are on television. The English actress gets to wear a long, sexy robe and, in a sultry voice, invites men to take their Viagra and come to bed. Then, after thirty seconds, along comes a Scottish actress singing and dancing in her car about overcoming her bladder problems with Tena underwear. I just dinna get it.

I would now like to invite Jim to present his Immortal Memory of Robert Burns. Please have something in your glass for some toasts when he is finished.

Immortal Memory

Adam is signing up for Apple iPhone service, turns to Eve, and asks, "Do I hae to read these terms and conditions?"

Did you hear about the thoughtful Scotsman who was heading out to the pub? He turned to his wee wife before leaving and said, "Jackie, put your hat and coat on lassie."

She replied, "Aww Iain that's nice. Are you taking me to the pub with you?"

"Nah, I'm just switching the central heating off while I'm oot."

A woman was counting nickels, dimes, and quarters on the kitchen table when she suddenly got very angry and started shouting and crying for no reason.

Her husband rushed out to the pub and told his buddy, "She's going through the change."

Walter went on a date with his new girlfriend, and they reached the door of her flat just before midnight. When she kissed him goodnight, she said, "Be careful on your way home, or someone might rob you of all the money you've saved this evening."

Have you heard about the lecherous Scotsman who lured a girl up to his attic to see his etchings? He sold her four of them.

Now, I would welcome Wally to give the Toast to the Lassies. We did have a dress rehearsal for this, and I told Wally just to look straight into the faces of all the pretty lassies. He did, got dizzy, and fell down, so we will try again. It's okay to smile at him, but please don't get him dizzy again.

"Who?" says God.

"Well, how about that Scots poet, Rabbie Burns?" says Jesus. "All the womenfolk loved him; he was popular with the boys in the pubs; and his poems were immortal."

God replies, "But look at the pain you went through. No one can suffer like that."

"What's a cross to bear?" says Jesus. "Hae you seen that Scots weather? Poor Burns was out in the rain at all hours, and he caught pneumonia and died that way. Is that no the worst?"

"Well, we'll gie it a try and see what happens," replied God.

And all of a sudden, there is Burns, on his first day back, sitting in a pub on Union Street in Traverse City having a pint. And this woman comes into the bar and sits beside him. She looks at Burns, still dressed in his Scottish eighteenth century clothes.

"What do you do?" she asks.

"I am a Scottish poet. I write long sonnets about the ladies. I tell them of my love for them." He then asks the woman about herself.

"I am a lesbian," she says. Burns stares, confused. She continues, "I love women. I like being close to them. I like to touch them, to smell them, and to be with them."

After a while she leaves, and a guy sits on her stool. He looks at Burns and asks, "What are you?"

Burns thinks, then says, "I used to think I was a poet."

We'd now like our society's president, Jim, to come up for some closing words and appreciation, and then we should all stand, form a circle, join hands, and sing "Auld Lang Syne" while Jane leads us on the concertina.

Appreciation

"Auld Lang Syne"

A few other jokes kept in reserve to insert at opportune times:

How do you tell what clan a Scotsman's from? Stick your hand up his kilt, and, if it's a quarter pounder, he's a MacDonald.

At an art auction in Edinburgh, Scotland, a wealthy American lost his wallet containing £20,000 [$28,000]. He announced to the gathering that he would give a reward of £200 to the person who found it. From the back of the hall, a Scottish voice shouted, "I'll give £250."

Winters can be extremely cold in northern Scotland, so the owner of the estate felt he was doing a good deed when he bought earmuffs for his farm worker, Archie.

Noticing, however, that Archie wasn't wearing the earmuffs even on the coldest day, the owner asked, "Didn't you like the earmuffs I gave you?"

Archie replied, not wishing to upset his employer, "Och, they are a wondrous thing."

"Then why don't you wear them?"

Archie explained, "I was wearing them the first day, but somebody offered to buy me a drink, and I didnae hear him."

Jock walks into a bar one day and stammers, "Does anyone here own that Doberman pinscher outside?"

"Yeah, I do," a tattooed biker says, standing up. "What about it?"

"Well, I think my little Scotty terrier just killed him."

"What are you talkin' about?" the biker says, disbelievingly. "How could your little runt kill my Doberman?"

"Well," mumbled Jock, "it appears that he got stuck in your dog's throat."

An elderly Scotsman goes into a chemist's shop. He says to the assistant, "I have a headache, have you any aspirin?"

"Certainly, sir," she replies. "Would you like fifty or 100?"

"No," the Scotsman says, "just the one. I've only got one headache."

"Address to a Haggis"

Traditional version

Fair fa' your honest, sonsie face,
Great Chieftain o' the Puddin-race!
Aboon them a' ye tak your place,
Painch, tripe, or thairm:
Weel are ye wordy of a grace
As lang's my arm.

The groaning trencher there ye fill,
Your hurdies like a distant hill,
Your pin wad help to mend a mill
In time o' need,
While thro' your pores the dews distil
Like amber bead.

His knife see Rustic-labour dight,
An' cut ye up wi' ready slight,
Trenching your gushing entrails bright,
Like onie ditch;
And then, O what a glorious sight,
Warm-reekin, rich!

Then, horn for horn, they stretch an' strive:
Deil tak the hindmost, on they drive,
Till a' their weel-swall'd kytes belyve